About the author

Leader. Wife. Mother. Friend. Poet. Mentor. Human. Shannon Moyer-Szemenyei is a believer in fundamental rights, standing up for oneself and being a kind and compassionate human being, leaving a positive impact wherever possible. Shannon lives with her family in London, Ontario and, when not writing or nurturing others, you can find her at the hockey rink or horse barn with her boys, or cuddled on the couch with her rescue dog, Berney.

THE YEARS OF BREAKING

SHANNON
MOYER-SZEMENYEI

THE YEARS OF BREAKING

Vanguard Press

VANGUARD PAPERBACK

© Copyright 2020
Shannon Moyer-Szemenyei

A CIP catalogue record for this title is
available from the British Library.

ISBN 9781784658137

*Vanguard Press is an imprint of
Pegasus Elliot MacKenzie Publishers Ltd.*
www.pegasuspublishers.com

First Published in 2020

**Vanguard Press
Sheraton House Castle Park
Cambridge England**

Printed & Bound in Great Britain

Dedication

To those who struggle to find their way, whose hearts are broken and souls are fragmented. This is for you.

Acknowledgements

The process of bringing *The Years Of Breaking* was nothing short of a facing a tornado head on. It was a process of deep healing, of growth, of pushing boundaries and of finding myself in the words that dripped from my pen on to the pages of my journals.

Through the process, my process of breaking, there are incredible human beings who stood by me, picking me up when I fell, reminding me of my worth, and who never gave up on me because they knew that I mattered and that these words mattered.

To my wonderful husband, Colin. Without you saying *I think something is wrong* that fall day, I wouldn't have taken the steps forward to figure out what was going on in my mind, which eventually would lead me back to the pages of my journal. Without you, I'm not sure I would have survived and overcome PTSD. Without you, I think the grief would have swallowed me. But it didn't, and because of you I remembered who I am at the core of my being, and I am grateful.

To my boys. My bear and my lion. Owen and Graeme. One day, I hope you look back on this time and see that your mom was strong. I hope you see that she never gave up, even when the world told her to. I hope you see how many lives she touched with the words from her pen. And I hope you see that you can do big things too, because you are extraordinary human beings.

To those who taught me to see the power in my voice, even when it was just a whisper. Jenn, Rachel, Tanya, Angela, Jena – I am forever grateful that you walked into my life at the exact moments that you did.

To Brynah, for the safety of your office, the time between sessions and the encouragement to keep going. For your unwavering belief that I could, and would, overcome PTSD and that it would one day release its hold on me. For your compassion, and your guidance. Thank you.

Lastly, to every single individual who shared their stories of trauma with me – I thank you. Your bravery has not gone unnoticed and has become woven in through these stories and words. Your stories are my stories, and mine are yours. She is me, I am her – we are all in this together. May you find healing, may you find peace. And may you know the life that is waiting for you on the other side of fear.

Be gentle with my soul, for it has been broken.
It has felt a grief so great that the breath has left my body
and touched the core of this earth.

And stayed there.

That breath, born from a soul so broken that it simply
could not return.

Be gentle with my soul, for a large piece of it is
missing.
It has been forever changed, in that one instant
where breath left my body, never to return.

My breath lingers there at the core of the earth.

Searching.
Seeking.
Waiting.

Be gentle with my soul. It is me and yet not. It is
learning how to be whole while waiting for my breath
to return.

Be gentle.
My soul aches.

I call you home.
From the edges of the earth, the places that are infinite and expansive.

I call you home.

From where time matters not, and moments last beyond comprehension.

I call you home.

Here in your body, aligned with your breath. Muscles aching and soul eternally etched on your heart.

I call you home.

Dig deep into the waters of your soul.

There is no place that will offer a sense of belonging, of home, than that within you.

Your soul. That little magical spark. The essence of your being. Your imprint of this world.

Dig deep and allow yourself to swim in its waters.
Bathe in its healing energy.
Breathe it in until you no longer feel as though you are a separate entity.

Merge your life force with your soul. Begin this process of coming home.

Your soul.
Your spark.
The essence of who you are.

You are home.

Of light and dark, I sit and I wait.
The discord within me,
such turbulence,
such anguish.

Deeply within, the light aches to be released.
This period of darkness simply cannot last forever.

Enough now.
Enough and grow silent, you dark and twisted mind.
This is not the life intended for me.

Let that brilliant light be free.
Allow it to magnify every piece of my being, stirring up
even the darkest spaces.

Be silent.
Be still.
Rest my wary soul in the magnitude of this space.

Let me breathe.

And then I covered my eyes, took a deep breath and finally, I could see.

The darkness brought a magnified clarity, an unexpected and vulnerable truth.

It fed my soul. It lit my spark.

A light grew from within. From behind my closed eyes.
Covered but not blind.
Awakened and reborn.

I covered my eyes. My breath hung in the air like a veil.

And finally, I could see.

Today, I begin again.
Just as I have so many times before.

This time, it feels different. There is a spark.
A flame.

Something deep within my soul is crying out.

It longs to be cared for.
To be cultivated.

My soul is tired and so too is my body and my mind.

Too long have I sought to be everything to everyone and
all I have achieved is a deep sense of loss.

Loss of self.
Loss of soul.

Today, I begin again.
With fire in my lungs and passion in my heart.

I begin to pull the pieces of myself back together.

Today.
Not tomorrow or the day after.

We gather in circle. Our voices strong and distinct, yet all somehow telling the same story.

Words we don't want to have to say
but our truth
nonetheless.

Words of actions that hold us captive within our own bodies.
Our minds.
Our souls.

We are not to blame. We did not ask for this. We did not want this to be our truth.

We did not consent.

We did not.
We would not.

We gather in circles. We rise up and share our stories. We take our power back and we say not again.

And so she loved.

While the rest of the universe told her not to.

While others sought to sew seeds of doubt.

She loved.
Deeply and with reckless abandon.

Without agenda or need for answers.
Fully and completely.

And so she loved.
Herself.

I send my breath down.
Down into the depths of my soul.

Down.
Deep down
to where my fears reside.

As my breath lingers here, it strains to find hope. It feels
lost in the despair that breeds from my fear.

And yet I sent it there.

Down.
Deep down.

Knowing that the only way out is through, and that
through means facing these fears.

The process is just unfolding, each breath uncovering a
new layer.

So I will send it down.
Deep down.

To linger. To wait.
To sit. And to heal.

Down into the depths of my soul.

The rain gently falls, each drop ripe with the promise of a new start.

What lies behind me, the path I took to where I stand now, is but a memory. A fleeting moment in time.

The fears I once had, the apprehension and doubt, they're gone.
Almost as if the rain has washed them away and muddied the path I took to get here.

All that matters is what lies before me.
The richness of new beginnings, the promise of prosperity and growth.

These things I invite with open arms.

The wind blows and the rain falls gently, signalling a change.

It is time.

Let me rest.
Let me just be.
My body aches and my soul is weary.

I can barely breathe. I need space, need to rest.

I send an invitation to sleep, to wrap me up in the safety
and comfort it provides.

My body aches.
My soul is weary.

Need to rest.
Need to rest.

Few things in life scare me more than the thought of not being here anymore.

Breath gets caught in my throat.
Heart beats a little faster.

And I'm paralyzed.

I can't move.

Yet I go through the most ordinary and mundane tasks.

Living
but afraid to die.

It happens when I think too long.
Drive past a cemetery.
Let myself linger.

It keeps me captive. Holds my breath tight and won't let go.

This crippling sense of fear.

How much time is left?
What comes after?
Will I know?

It's all too much to bear.
So I stay afraid.
Barely breathing.

Living
but afraid to die.

I take comfort in the dark.

Yesterday, I was terrified.
The fear was crippling.
I couldn't breathe.

But today the darkness is familiar and safe, like an old friend.

It feels comfortable here, albeit sad.

Deeply sad.
In my bones kind of sad.

But there's a level of comfort here in the dark. An unspoken trust.

Though it's safe and comfortable here in the dark, there isn't much living going on.

The thought of living is what makes it hard to breathe.
To throw caution to the wind, to be reckless and just live.

So, for now, I'll stay here in the dark where it is warm and safe.

Just for now.
Here in the dark.

All at once, the magnitude hit me like a wave.
A wave crashing down with such force that I had no time to prepare or recover.

Today.
This date.
It catches me off guard, yet I always know it's coming.

The wave hits, and I'm pulled under.
I can't breathe and there's no use fighting.

My heart breaks.
It shatters into a million pieces, my soul seeping out between the cracks.

Today.
This date.
It makes my bones ache, my body hurt.
The magnitude of losing you, crashing down on me like a wave.

It hits over and over, and I feel the wave starting to swell as the date draws near.

It's almost over.
Just hold on.
I'll spend a year putting the pieces back together, only for it to hit again.

Screaming *stop*, but bracing for impact.

Breath caught in my throat.
Mind blank but racing at the same time.

Unable to move, yet scrambling to get out of the way.

Walking away, unscathed, but trembling inside.

Sobbing.
Breaking.

Yet sitting still and whole.

The sun spreads warmth across my body.
In this moment, here in the stillness of my breath, I return.

Back from the shadows, from behind the veil.

To stand in the sun, closing my eyes and just breathing.

Welcoming it back, down into my bones.
Giving life to my passions and creativity.

Giving life and balancing my soul.

Solitude.
The complete comfort of being alone.

Silence.
Quiet.
Dark.

My breath lingering at each passing minute.
Comfortable in the stillness.
Comfortable in the quiet.

Solitude.
Sweet solitude.

Silence.
Quiet.
Alone.

Do not tell me not to weep.
On a day, where loss feels insurmountable, when tears
pool and hearts break.

Do not tell me not to cry.
Do not tell me not to be angry.
Do not tell me it is better.
Do not tell me not to weep.

Hearts are breaking.
Lives are ripped apart.

The air outside grows cold and the wind whips through the trees.

It's time for the world to darken.
To draw its blinds, batten the hatches and grow quiet.

Still.
Dark.
Quiet.

Nothing needs tending to but the fire that burns within.

The secret plans.
This is the time of the great winter sleep where we turn inward.

And listen.

As the words were read, his shoulders rose and fell, signalling to everyone that he was breaking.

You have to take care of him, she said. *He's going to be lonely now.*

She was gone.
His heart was broken.

For him, I weep. My soul aches and my heart reaches out to comfort, knowing it can never mend what is broken.

She is gone.
His heart is broken.

The silence and stillness that come from deep reflection.

The want to turn inward, to listen, to hush.

Silence calls to me. It beckons me home and in some way illuminates my very being.

It lights a flame and there in the shadow, I recognize myself.

Hiding no more.
Stepping bravely into the light.
Silent and still, held in reflection.

Sometimes I sit in wonder.
This life.

What is it meant for if one day it all comes to an end?

Why was I chosen to walk this path that I do not understand?

Why this?
Why me?

The thoughts drown me in sorrow and panic, like waves crashing down.

This life.
Why?
Why me?

Those gripping fears are clawing at me again.

Clawing and wanting to sink their teeth into my flesh.

Scratching at the surface of my skin and trying to break through.

Fear.

What a funny thing.
Completely made up in my mind and founded in no element of concrete proof.

And yet there is it, planting seeds of doubt and thoughts of despair.

Holding me hostage.
Clawing at my skin.

The need to be wanted. To feel like I'm taking his breath away.

Desired.
Attractive.

Passionately wanted.

But, ignored.

So coldly ignored, and then scolded for feeling.

For wanting. For expressing.

Still needing to be wanted.
To be desired.

Yet withdrawn and ignored.

It felt like opening a wound, but it was necessary.

My words.
My experience.
My sweet, sweet arrow.

It happened so others can heal.

So they can grieve.
So they can find peace.

The bandages have been removed.
The wound is open, breathing in fresh air.

It's time to heal.

Today I choose to walk through the fire.
No longer fearing the risk of being burned.
I choose to stand up for what is right and to use my voice.

No longer will I be made to feel less than.
I am capable.
So capable and confident.
I know where I am headed and with the purest of intentions, I am no longer willing to sit back and let the fire consume me.

I walk through the fire, needing no shield and no protection.

Today, the fire fears me.

I am a force to be reckoned with.
I will not be silent.
I will not be still.

Fear me, for today I choose to fight.

My anger felt like a spiral and I was at the centre.

Angry for things that I could not control.
For things lost
and things unknown.

I gave my power over to the anger.
I let it capture my breath and hold me hostage.

Since losing you, it's been the only thing that has
stayed consistent.

People and places have come and gone. But the anger
has always stayed.

A spiral.
It's more like a tornado.
A complete cyclone of chaos.

In the middle. Always in the middle.

Will I ever gain control?
Will it always consume me?

I am safe and I am grounded.

Here within my body, my breath travels down and dissolves my fears.

They cannot hold me captive.

I choose to rise.

I belong and I am worthy.

My body provides safe shelter to my soul, my breath.

I am not lacking.
With my breath, I let go of fear and trust that I am eternally safe.

Deeply rooted and deeply connected.

My body calls me home.

I wrote your story today.

These words that I've been clinging to.
This notion that if I truly express how it felt to grieve
for you that somehow it would mean a piece of you
would stay as a distant memory.

The fact is, I am forever changed because of you.

I called you by name.
And not the one that we've grown to call you, but your
real, honest, pure and beautiful name.

I wrote your story today.

And my heart didn't shatter. Somehow, the broken
pieces were mended together when I started to write.

I called you by name.
I wrote your story.

When no words come, I wonder why.

Is there something wrong?
Surely, I have some thought or feeling that needs to be
processed.

And then it clicks.

What if, right here, right now, I am okay?

What if things have shifted,
darkness has lifted
and we are finally stepping into the light?

And there they are, the words.

Words of hope.
Words of light.

Deep into the heart.
The heart of my soul.
To be heard,
to feel.

Deep into the magnitude of the larger expanse of my
being.

To grow,
to achieve.

Deep into the solitude.
The solitude of my breath and my body.
To draw inward,
to come home.

Deep into the heart.
The heart of my soul.
To be heard,
to feel.

We walk through together.

We struggle together
and we are rising together.

Reflection is a funny thing.
Often, it refers to mirror work. Of looking at oneself and typically not liking what we see.

Turning away instead of turning in.

Hiding.
Loathing.

Yet now reflection seems to be a moment of pause.
Of deep thought and inquiry.

The reflection I see now is of the steps taken toward purpose.

Of a foundation that needed tending to, a heart that needed mending.

As I reflect, I see the broken pieces and recognize them as necessary elements.

I had to break so that I could rebuild.

Reflection has led me to a purpose and to feeling whole.

New.
Built.
Strong.

The process of reflecting has given each word and each moment new purpose.

I see now that before, I was somewhat just going through the motions.

Reflection has led to purpose.
Reflection has led to being more mindful of moments, breath, words and movement.

I crumbled so I could rise.
I broke so I could grow.

I reflect so I can push forward with intention.

These moments of discovery and this process of writing. It has been tremendously healing for my soul.

And while I still have so very much to learn, while I know that I have barely scratched the surface.
The words come without want.
The come and they beg to be written without being forced.

The just come.

The emotions that stir, thoughts and experiences long buried.
They just come.

They just come.

It's as if I've reached down deep into my soul, with no expectation, and dipped my pen into its well.

The ink is the blood that runs in my veins.

And the words just come.

It's been a while since I last put pen to paper.

The thoughts have grown dark once more and I feel the cycle of solitude creeping in.

Perhaps it is the hustle and bustle of the season.

Or perhaps this is just who I am.

A person afraid.
Afraid of dying, of losing control.

A person who needs proof in so many ways,
yet one who is creative and expressive and lives fully in her heart.

Troubled in many ways.
Confused.
Maybe lost.

Afraid of the after and never fully in the now.

So close to the end, and yet feeling so small.

It's an odd place to find yourself in, and one that brings much worry.

Often feeling like an outsider looking in.
Just observing and here for but a moment.

So close to the end, but so small.
So young.
So afraid.

I see little pockets of light, and I can't help but wonder
if it's you.

Little flashes that linger in the air, almost like
luminescent bubbles.

They're gone as quickly as they appear.

And I can't help but wonder,
is it you?

A fresh start.
A new page.

Finally ready to lay the demons to rest and take back the power.

I know fear will come, and so too will the feelings spiral.

But.
But.

I will take back my power and intentionally choose to breathe.

To live.
To run wild and free.

And to not be held back by fear.

It has held me captive for far too long.

No more.

I've never really called my fear by name.
Strangely by naming it,
I feel like its power lessens somehow.

Death.

The fear of not being here.
Of not being able to embrace my children,
feel the warmth of their skin.

When I spend time thinking about those moments, my
heart races and I am overcome with fear.

Death.

Not the actual death but the being taken away.

I call my fear by name.
I say it out loud and ask to be released.

A year of breaking, or at least that's how it felt.

Breaking.
Shaking.
Rebuilding.

Being challenged right down to my fundamental values
and feeling broken.

And not just like chipped or cracked.
But completely shattered.

I look back on the year that we leave behind and realize
that each moment I fell apart.

Each moment that left me broken, all of them.

Messy.
Ugly.
Anxious.
Full of fear and panic.

A year of breaking was essential to my growth.

And now I rise.

The dull ache resurfaces, reminding me that my body was broken.

Thoughts long buried.
Images played out in slow motion.

And yet if I or he had been moving just a bit faster, that ache wouldn't be here.

I would be gone.

Too long of a pause but the words just haven't been there.

Nothing begging to be written.
No sage words of wisdom.

No pain to work through.

Possibly it means I'm more present,
more aware.

Or maybe it just means that I'm growing numb.

My heart aches for her.

She doesn't understand the implications of her actions or the impending fallout.

She doesn't see the pain coming.

While the holding onto hope is admirable, I worry.

I ache for her.

She, deserving of happiness and joy, but not seeing her true worth.

Settling. Always settling.

Never fully taking time to sit with herself and get to know what she truly wants.

She doesn't understand.
She doesn't see it.

But I do
and I ache.

Just waiting.

Completely confused and feeling defeated.

I had a handle on this.

Everything was working perfectly.
I felt new, reborn and completely like myself.

And now?

It feels as if all of that has been undone.

I'm lost.
I'm confused.
And I'm breaking.

She was broken.

Very simply put.
She was broken and the wounds were so raw that it felt
like her flesh was on fire.

No more hiding.
No more masking the pain.

Time to feel every ugly and horrible ounce of it.

She was broken.

I'm done.

I've sat in silence and allowed myself to be...

Bullied.
Made to feel less than.
Disrespected.

And for what?

I am stronger than that and my life has more value than
what is wrapped up in one pretentious person's opinion.

Hear me roar.
There is only so long that I can stay silent.

Stay hidden.
Keep up with appearances.
Be proper.

No more.
I am done.

My voice demands to be heard, for it is powerful and
perfectly valid.

It's your turn to sit,
grow silent
and shrivel into yourself.

Hear me, for I will not be silent.

Days of silence.
Followed by small talk that feels unnatural and forced.

What are we doing?
This isn't us.

The silence is uncomfortable.
The small talk, insignificant.

Maybe the silence is necessary.
Maybe the small talk is what you need.

How can it be, though?
How can the very root of our relationship be reduced to
small talk and messages left unanswered?

Just because we can't agree?
Because I see your worth, your pain, your fight, and am
willing to say...

You matter?
You're important?
You deserve better?

Because I wouldn't be silent and turn a blind eye to the
reality of the situation and demand better for you?

I just can't be silent.
And that doesn't mean that I don't care.
Or that I'm not here.

In reality, it's the exact opposite.

I worry.
In the very depths of my soul, I worry about you.
Your perception of your worth.

You may not see it, but the most supportive thing I can do is use my voice.
Demand better.

But for now, the silence and small talk ensues.

It is cold.
I don't like it.

This isn't us.

I don't quite understand.
I didn't ask for things to be this way, and yet somehow the blame is being placed squarely on my shoulders.

The guilt is manifesting.
The confusion setting in.

But no.
Hold on.

The event didn't happen as you say.

I tried.
I came from a place of love and compassion.

But your hurt and your trouble clouds your judgment.
You push and push, but I still remain here at your side.

I tried.
I am still trying.

But you need to, too.

She was shining.
The world had tried to consume her but it failed.

Tried and failed.

Her light was simply too bright.
It could not be extinguished.

She fought for the ground on which she stands.
Her battle cry a tiny whisper because she knows that her
presence is enough.

Enough.
So enough.

Her light.
Her whisper.
Always enough.

Climbing up out of darkness only to be met with a barrier.
The light of beyond calling to me, but unreachable.

Pushing, it pulsating.
One run, one moment of strength and the wall shatters like glass.

Falling on the other side,
and staring at your face.

The message abundantly clear and piercing my heart.

You have everything you need.

And then comfortable there in the silence.

Covered in silver.
Bathed in light.

I am all that I need.

Take care of my tender heart.

I give each day until there is nothing left.
And then I find a few more ounces to give some more.

Each moment and breath is spent
tending
worrying
caring
loving
helping
nurturing
someone else.

Every last drop poured into something, someone else.

But I need tending to.

My heart needs rest, and my soul needs a safe place to
come home to.

This time, it is me that needs the care and the love.
The nurturing of someone close.

The drops poured back in so that I can give once more.

Take care of my tender heart, for I need rest.

You had no idea, but you broke me.

The one person, my person, who I have always relied on.

You broke me.

And I think what's worse is that you did so because you are hurt and you are broken.

But instead of owning, growing, learning and reflecting, you needed someone to blame.

You picked me.
I was the easy target and the logical choice simply because you knew that no matter how much you hurt me, I would stay.

You knew that if you needed me, I would put everything aside for you.

When you hurt, I hurt.

But this is killing me.
This is breaking me.

You are shattering every fibre of my being and instead of owning it, you twist it.

I can accept the hurt I've caused.
The pain my worry and concern have inflicted.

Can you not see the compassion it is so heavily drenched in?

I guess the why matters not.
Because you ache.
You are hurt.
You are angry.

So you break me.

What is it that makes my soul heavy?
What prevents me from truly living?
From breathing?

Limitations
Judgment
Fear
Guilt

All things that are fabricated and manifest in my mind
during the darkest hours.

This is my process of letting go.
Of reclaiming my power.
Of taking back the control.

The burdens of fear.
The weight of limitations.
Even the expectations I put on myself and the amount
that I give.

I need this weight to lift.
I need to be free.

To breathe.
To grow.
To live.

You talk in circles,
but this time I refuse to chase you.

I have spoken my piece,
explained my side and all I can do now is hope that one
day you will understand my words.
And accept your part in this.

But I will not chase you.
My bones and my heart are heavy and my soul is tired.

Run yourself in circles, but know that this time you run
alone.

My body has not been my own.
It has been someone else's
experience
property
playground
thing.
Until recently.
Recently I have stepped in, reclaimed and said no.

No more will I allow my body to be for someone else.
No more will my body be defined by someone else's
ideals and images.

No.

My body is my home.
It has curves and sass.
It is strong and it has borne life.

But it hasn't always been this way.

I've been at war with myself.
I've been lost.

But finally, I come home.
I reclaim my body and it is mine.

Right here in this moment, my body feels fluid and strong.

Capable and confident.

Each muscle, each breath connecting and speaking to one another.

My body feels alive, ignited.

Fluid and strong.
Capable and confident.
Fully aware and alive.

How many months?
I seem to have lost track.

Sweet melody in my ears and yet pain in my heart.

I didn't realize how much healing there was still to do.

I didn't realize the storm that was brewing and just how it would surface.

The fire burning hot in my veins and the need to unleash it.

I couldn't hold back anymore, and what a beautiful moment of chaos it was.

A moment to stand tall against Goliath and use my voice.

A moment to inspire the healing to begin.

Then to sit back,
grow comfortable in the discomfort
and watch the choices unfold.

Three months have passed.
Actually, almost to the day.

Each day in between I have worked.
I have searched.
I have healed and I have grown.

I am the storm.
I am the chaos.

Standing tall against Goliath.
Hear my words and feel my fire.

Heal and grow.
Become comfortable with the discomfort.
Shift and change.

Heal this pain.

A constant process of begin, then begin again.

Starting over.

Even going backward in time.
Facing demons long since bottled and tucked away.

Naive to think that the healing process comes to a close
and that we can move on.

Foolish to bottle those demons,
store them on a shelf,
turn off the light
and close the door.

They always come back.

And each time they do,
they are a little stronger,
more violent,
louder and angrier.

It's been a month since I've started over,
again.

Facing demons, one by one
and doing the work so that no bottles, shelves, lights or
doors are required.

Going backward into the deep recesses of my mind to begin again.

Body ever changing.
An evolution into itself.

A process of unfolding,
unpacking.
Breaking down and breaking apart.

I am whole and yet not.
Made of parts that don't always make sense.

I evolve.
I shift and I change.

Sometimes resisting.
Other times inviting those changes, that growth.

I am whole and yet not.

I always needed you but knew you didn't have the capacity to care.

You were there, yet not.

A ghost.
One that haunts me still.
One that I can't seem to rid myself of no matter how hard I try.

How you can constantly put him first...

Do you not see the pain you are causing?

I've come to understand that these relationships we
think we should have, allegiances to our blood,
are ones that are thrust upon us and ones that we are
made to feel guilty about should we choose to walk
away.

But I choose to walk away.

I'm tired of hurting and for me to move forward, I have
to be done with this.
I can't keep alternating between
hurt,
anguish,
grief,
pain,
anger,
frustration
and disbelief.

It's confusing.
It's haunting.
And it's toxic.

I may be last to you, but to me I am first.

My soul is tired.
My eyes unable to cry, yet my heart is shattering into a million pieces.

I should know better by now.
Should know not to obsess over that which I can't control and can't change.

I should know better than to think you will call,
that you will care.

I should know, but for some reason I hold out hope.

Hope that will never be answered.

Hope that will just turn into disappointment.

Into heartbreak.

Into grief.

For a moment there, I forgot who I was.

I would look in the mirror and see a shell of who I had been.
A complete stranger.
Someone I didn't even recognize.

But I felt a pull.
A pull to find out who she was.
What she knew.
Where she had been.
All along feeling like she was me and I was her.

Peeling back the layers, one by one.
Breaking apart.
Falling down.
Uncovering the mysteries of my own soul.

And there I was.

Uncertain and afraid.
Beaten and broken.
Heart bleeding and left to mother herself.

Her world ripped apart when her father died and, along with him, the remnant of the only family she had known. Left to fend for herself.

Left.

No wonder she had gotten lost along the way.

Grieving you has become exhausting.

And confusing.

It's like purgatory.

I grieve and come to terms with the loss of something that was never really there, and then a glimmer of hope pulls me back in.

I feel stuck and I don't know how to get free.

Do not dismiss me.

Do not try to quiet me
when fire is running through my veins

and a tornado is brewing in my throat.

Did you even know he touched me?
Or did you forget that too?

I know I told you.
I know you heard me.

So why do you stand by his side, like my words don't
even matter?

Why do you choose him?

Why do I expect anything different?

Why is it that we turn a blind eye and a deaf ear to those
who speak out and say...

He hurt me.

I was too young to understand.

It should never have happened, but it did.

So why do you choose him when he's the one who
caused the hurt?

They didn't believe me.

I was screaming at the top of my lungs and they didn't believe me.

He choked me.
Threw me against a wall.

And they didn't believe me.

Instead, we sat in a room, me telling stories of what had happened.

And they didn't believe me.

Years later, the stories would resurface and the pain would return.

And still, they didn't believe me.

He broke me.
I lost everything because of him.

And they don't believe me.

Would they believe me if I said I was eight?
That I didn't understand that it wasn't okay?

Sweatpants and a sweatshirt.
Pale pink, if memory serves.

Years later, jeans and a t-shirt.

In high school, cargo pants and a raglan tee.

Then my prom dress.

Would they believe me if I said I was twenty?
That I laid there, helpless and alone,
pretending to sleep?

A patchwork denim skirt and a white button-down shirt.
Black platforms and navy blue bra.

Black dress pants and a white shirt. The same one as
before.

Would they believe me if I said it happened six times?

That each time broke my spirit just a little bit more?

Would they believe me then?

You're so brave, they say.

The truth is, I am terrified.

I am terrified of the words reaching the wrong ears.

That somehow my speaking up, that my breaking, will haunt instead of heal.

The truth is, it's not about being brave or being strong.

It's about being honest.
It's about finding peace.
It's about doing what's right.

And using my voice to that others can heal.

The flood gates are open.

There's no going back now.

What a bold statement.

To tell someone that you are always there,
when the truth is you never have been.

What a ridiculous facade.

Showing the world a relationship that has never existed.

And yet to call you out on it,
to even reply with a pleasantry,
seems like it just perpetuates the lie,
yet causes further hurt.

It feels like living in limbo,
continuing the fallacy.

What a bold statement.

You've never been there.

It's exhausting being at war with someone who doesn't even acknowledge the battle.

Who doesn't have the capacity to care.

At some point, surrender seems inevitable.
Necessary, even, if I am to survive.

My heart has grown numb.
My body weak and my mind tired of the constant fight.

The inner battle of needing to be heard,
and knowing that you can't.

To be seen,
and knowing that you can't,

To be loved,
and knowing that you can't.

So I surrender.
This is me letting go and choosing my own survival as more important than the battle with you.

The war is done.
The battle is over.

·

CPSIA information can be obtained
at www.ICGtesting.com
Printed in the USA
BVHW030841260720
584579BV00001B/64